D1226702

PILGRIM'S
PROGRESS

ILLUSTRATIONS BY KEITH CRISS

PILGRIM'S PROGRESS

AS RETOLD BY MACK THOMAS

JOHN BUNYAN

GOLD 'N' HONEY FAMILY CLASSICS

j823
Bun

I run in the path of your commands,
for you have set my heart free.

PSALM 119:32

PILGRIM'S PROGRESS

published by Gold'n'Honey Books
a part of the Questar publishing family

© 1996 by Questar Publishers, Inc.
Illustrations © 1996 by Keith Criss
Designed by David Uttley

International Standard Book Number: 0-88070-917-0

Printed in Mexico

ALL RIGHTS RESERVED
No part of this publication may be reproduced, stored in a retrieval system,
or transmitted, in any form or by any means—electronic, mechanical,
photocopying, recording, or otherwise—without prior written permission.

For information:
Questar Publishers, Inc., Post Office Box 1720
Sisters, Oregon 97759

96 97 98 99 00 01 02 03 — 10 9 8 7 6 5 4 3 2 1

1499

TABLE OF  CONTENTS

While walking in a forest I found a cave,
where I lay down to sleep.
And as I slept, I dreamed a dream...

SEEKING HIS FORTUNE

I N MY DREAM I saw a man in rags standing outside his house. A huge burden was on his back. He was reading a book, and sobbing and shaking. "What should I do?" he cried.

At last he went inside. He was quiet, wanting to hide his trouble from his family. But he couldn't stay silent long. "Oh, dear wife!" he burst out. "And my own children! This burden is breaking me! And now I've learned for certain that fire from heaven will destroy our town. We'll all be burned up! Unless — somehow — we can find a way of escape."

His wife and children were shocked — not because they believed his words, but because they thought his mind was terribly sick. Since night was coming, they thought some sleep would settle him down. They helped him to bed. But he spent all night moaning and weeping.

In the morning they asked how he felt. "Worse," he answered. He repeated what he said the day before, but his wife and children didn't care to hear it. They scolded him, then made fun of him.

Finally they ignored him. So he went into his bedroom to pray for them.

The next few days he often walked alone in the fields nearby, reading sometimes and sometimes praying. In his trouble he would cry out again, "What should I do to be saved?"

Once he thought about running away. But which way would he run?

Then a man named Evangelist came up to him and asked, "Why do you cry?"

"I understand from this book," he answered, "that I'm to die, and then be judged. I don't want to die."

"Why not," Evangelist said, "since this life has so many troubles?"

"I'm afraid this burden on my back will sink me into the place that burns with fire," the man answered. "I'm not fit to be judged. Just thinking about it makes me weep."

"Then why are you just standing here?" Evangelist said.

"Because I don't know where to go."

Evangelist gave him a sheet of paper. On it the man read these words: "Run away, for God's anger is coming!"

He looked carefully at Evangelist. "Where should I run?"

Evangelist pointed across a wide field. "Do you see that narrow gate?"

"No."

"Then do you see that shining light?"

"I think so."

"Keep it in sight," Evangelist said. "Go straight for it, then you'll see the gate. Knock at it, and you'll be told what to do."

So the man began to run.

From his house, his wife and children saw him. "Come back!" they called. But he pressed his fingers to his ears and hurried toward the light. "Life!" he shouted. "Oh, life that will last forever!" He never looked back.

Two of his neighbors — one named Obstinate, and the other Pliable — went after the man. He was far ahead, but Obstinate and Pliable soon caught up. They told him he should come back with them.

"I can't!" he answered. "This town is the City of Destruction. Whoever stays here will sink lower than the grave, to a place burning with fire and lightning. Please, good neighbors, go with me!"

"What!" said Obstinate. "And leave behind our friends and all the good things we have?"

"Yes!" answered the man — whose name was Christian. "Yes indeed," said Christian, "because nothing you leave behind is worth comparing with even the tiniest part of what *I'm* going after. There's more than enough for all of us to share. Go with me and prove it!"

"But what exactly are you going after?" Obstinate asked.

"I seek my fortune," Christian answered. "A perfect fortune that can never be lost or spoiled or changed. It's waiting in heaven for anyone who goes after it. Here, read about it in my book."

"Oh, tush!" said Obstinate. "Away with your book. Will you come back with us, or not?"

"No," Christian answered. "I've put my hand to the plow."

Obstinate drew back. "Then come, neighbor Pliable," he said. "We'll return home without this crazy rooster-head."

"Don't be so rough on him," said Pliable. "If what good Christian says is true, he'll find better things than what we have here. My heart wants to go with my neighbor."

"What!" shouted Obstinate. "Another fool? Listen to me, Pliable: Who knows where this brain-sick fellow will lead you? Come back!"

"No, Pliable!" pleaded Christian. "Go with me, your neighbor! There's even more glory to be had than what I've told you. If you don't believe me, read it in my book. It's all guaranteed by the blood of the one who wrote it."

Pliable made up his mind to go with Christian. "But," he said, "do you know the way to this wonderful place?"

"A man named Evangelist directed me to a gate not far away," Christian assured him. "We'll get more instructions there."

Pliable smiled. "Let's go!"

Now in my dream I saw them leave Obstinate behind. They talked together while crossing a large field.

"I'm glad you're with me," said Christian. "Obstinate would never turn his back on us if only he knew the terrible things that are coming."

"Well, neighbor," Pliable said, "now that it's just the two of us, tell me more about what we'll enjoy in the place we're going."

Christian smiled. "I'll read it to you from my book."

"But do you know for sure the words in that book are true?"

"Yes," said Christian. "It was written by one who cannot lie."

Christian read to him about an endless kingdom where they could live forever. "We'll be given crowns of glory, and clothes to wear that make us shine like the sun!"

"I like that," said Pliable. "What else?"

"There'll be no more crying or sadness, because the owner of the place will wipe away every tear. You'll see angels to dazzle your eyes. And we'll be with everyone who went there before us, all of them loving and good. They're always in God's care, and he's glad to have them there forever. Some of them on earth were cut to pieces or burned or eaten by wild animals or drowned, all because of their love for the Lord. But now that they're with him, they can never die."

"My heart beats faster just hearing it," said Pliable. "How do we get to share in all this?"

"He tells us how in this book. He says if we're truly willing to have it all, then he'll give it to us for free."

"Oh, my good partner," said Pliable, "let's go faster!"

"I can't go as fast as I'd like," Christian said, "because of this burden on my back."

Now in my dream I saw them approach a swampy bog. It was called the Slough of

Despond. Suddenly, without watching, they both fell in. They wallowed in it, and were quickly coated with mud and muck.

"Neighbor Christian!" snorted Pliable. "Where are we now?"

"Truly," Christian blurted out, "I don't know!"

Pliable grew angry. "Is this the happiness you told me about? If I ever get out of this mess alive, you can have your new country all to yourself!"

With a desperate tumble he finally pulled himself out. Back he went across the field they had crossed, until he was out of Christian's sight.

Alone, Christian worked his way to the far side of the Slough. But he found it impossible to pull himself out.

Under his burden, he began to sink.

UP A FIERY MOUNTAIN

UT I SAW in my dream that as Christian struggled in the Slough, a man came up whose name was Help.

"What are you doing here?" he asked.

Christian sputtered, "A man called Evangelist sent me to a narrow gate in this direction, so I could escape God's coming anger. And on my way, I fell in here."

"Why didn't you look for the steps?"

But Christian had been running too scared to see some sturdy steps built out across the middle of the Slough.

"Give me your hand," said Help. He drew Christian out, and set him on solid ground.

As Christian went onward, I myself stepped over to his rescuer. "Sir," I asked, "why doesn't someone fill in this Slough, so poor travelers from the City of Destruction can go to the gate in safety?"

"This place cannot be mended," he answered. "When sinners overflow with filthy fears and dirty doubts, it all runs together and drains down into this miry Slough. Of course the King isn't pleased with that. For hundreds of years he's been sending workers to fill it in with the best materials. But the Slough has swallowed at least twenty thousand wagonloads of it. Millions of good and wholesome teachings have been brought from all over the King's dominion to be poured in here. But this place is still the Slough of Despond.

"Even those good steps the Lawgiver built can sometimes hardly be seen because of the vapors spewing up. But the ground is good once travelers get past the gate."

Now in my dream I saw Christian crossing a field. To one side he saw someone walking, and coming closer.

His name was Mr. Worldly Wiseman. He lived in the town of Carnal Policy, a large town close to where Christian was from.

Coming near, this man guessed who Christian was. Everyone had been talking about how he ran away.

"Good fellow," the man called, "where are you going in such a burdensome manner, sighing and groaning?"

"Burdensome manner is right," answered Christian, "as burdensome as any poor creature ever had. I'm going to a narrow gate over yonder. And there, I'm told, I'll be shown how to get rid of this burden. I can't get it off myself, and no one in our country can lift it from my shoulders."

"Who told you to take this path you're on?" asked Mr. Worldly Wiseman.

"A man who appeared great and honorable," Christian answered. "His name is Evangelist."

"Will you listen to me," Mr. Worldly Wiseman whispered, "if I give you advice?"

"I will if it's good," said Christian. "I need good counsel."

"Then I tell you: I curse this man for the instructions he gave you! There's no more dangerous or troublesome way in the world than this path he sent you on. You'll find it out yourself if you let him control you. I see already you've met with trouble — that mud all over you is from the Slough of Despond, which is only the beginning of the sorrows facing everyone who comes this way.

"Listen to me, for I'm older than you. In this direction, you're headed only for tiredness, pain, hunger, nakedness, sword, lions, dragons, and darkness — in a word, nothing but *death*. Everybody knows it. So why kill yourself by listening to that stranger?"

"But sir," Christian said, "this weight on my back is more terrible to me than anything you've mentioned. I don't care what I meet with, as long as I'm set free from this burden."

"How did you get it in the first place?"

"By reading this book."

"I thought so," said Mr. Worldly Wiseman. "You're like other weak men I know who meddle in things too high for them. It makes them run desperately and dangerously, with no idea what they're after."

"But I know what I'm after," said Christian: "To be free from my burden."

"Then why go down this path, with all its dangers? Especially since, if you'd just be patient and listen, I can show you how to get what you want without all the trouble. You'll find safety, friendship, and happiness."

Christian stepped closer. "Oh, sir," he said, "open this secret to me!"

The man smiled. "A mile away is a village named Morality. In it there lives a gentleman called Legalism, a man with good sense and a good name. He's helped many with burdens like yours to shed them off their shoulders. He can also cure their minds which have gone crazy from their burden. So go there at once. If perchance he isn't home, he has a handsome son named Good-Manners who can fix you up as fine as the old gentleman could."

"Sir," said Christian, "which way is this honest man's house?"

Mr. Worldly Wiseman pointed to a hill. "Go over that rise," he said. "The first house you come to will be his."

So Christian left his path and set out for the hill. As he reached it and began climbing, it grew higher and steeper. Christian soon began to fear the mountain would come crashing over on his head. He dug in his heels to keep from falling.

Suddenly flashes of fire leaped out from the hillside. Christian was sure he would now be burned. He stood sweating and shaking with fear, having no idea what to do.

And his burden now seemed heavier than ever.

AN OPEN DOOR

HRISTIAN NOW was truly sorry he had taken Mr. Worldly Wiseman's advice.

Then along the flaming hillside he saw Evangelist coming to meet him. His face looked stern and dreadful.

Christian blushed with shame.

"What are you doing here, Christian?" said Evangelist.

Christian didn't know how to answer. He stood speechless.

"Aren't you the man I found crying just outside the City of Destruction?" Evangelist asked.

"Yes sir. I'm the man."

"Didn't I direct you on the pathway to the narrow gate?"

"Yes, dear sir."

"You're off that path. Why did you turn away from it so quickly?"

Christian told all about Mr. Worldly Wiseman's advice, and how he followed it.

"Stand still a moment," said Evangelist, "so I can show you the words of God."

Christian stood trembling.

"See to it," Evangelist said, "that you listen to the one who speaks. If others could not escape when they ignored God's warning on earth, how can you escape if you turn your back on God's warning from heaven? For God says, 'My true child has life by believing me. But if he turns back, I will not be pleased with him.' Christian, you've run into misery because you rejected the counsel of the Most High God."

Christian dropped to the ground as if dead. "How terrible!" he cried. "I'll be destroyed!"

Evangelist reached down and helped him up. "All kinds of sins are forgiven," he said. "Stop doubting, and believe."

Christian felt better, but he still trembled as before.

"Listen carefully to what I tell you," Evangelist continued. "Mr. Worldly Wiseman is rightly named. He loves only what this world teaches, instead of the way of the cross. There are three things about his advice that you must absolutely hate.

"First, you should hate how he turned you off the path leading to the gate, and how you agreed to leave it. For the Lord says, 'Do your best to enter through the narrow gate.'

"Second, you should hate how he made you scorn the sufferings along your path. For the King says, 'Whoever tries to save his life will lose it.'

"Third, you should hate how he directed you into a different way leading only to death. That man named Legalism could never free you from your burden, for he himself is a slave and the son of a slave. This is his mountain, which you were afraid would fall on your head.

"So Mr. Worldly Wiseman is an alien, and Legalism is a cheat. As for his son Good-Manners, he may look pretty enough, but he's only a deceiver and could never give you help. Believe me, all the noise you've heard about these men is nothing but a plot to turn you from your salvation."

Evangelist looked up and called upon heaven to show the truth of his words. At once fire blasted out of the mountain beneath Christian's feet. It made his hair stand on end. He heard a voice say, "Anyone is doomed who thinks he can obey every law perfectly enough to live forever with God."

Christian now expected only death. He cried out in pain. He called himself a thousand fools for ever listening to Mr. Worldly Wiseman's advice.

He pleaded with Evangelist. "Sir, is there any hope for me? Can I go back and find the way to the narrow gate? Can my sin be forgiven?"

"Your sin is very great," answered Evangelist, "for by it you committed two evils: You

left the path that is good, and you went on the way that is forbidden. But the man at the gate will receive you, for he is your friend. Only take heed you don't turn aside again." Then Evangelist smiled, and hugged Christian, and wished him well.

Christian hurried down the hill and onward, saying nothing to anyone he met. He couldn't feel safe until he was back on the path for the gate.

And so, in time, he reached it. Above the gate was a sign reading, "Knock, and it shall be opened to you."

Christian knocked, again and again.

At last a serious-looking man came to the gate.

His name was Good Will. "Who are you?" he asked. "Where did you come from, and what do you want?"

Christian answered, "I'm a poor, burdened sinner. I come from the City of Destruction, but I go to Mount Zion, the Celestial City of God, that I may escape His coming anger. And since the way there goes through this gate, as I'm told, I want to know if you'll let me in."

"With all my heart," Good Will answered, and he opened it. "An open door is set before you, and no man can shut it."

Christian stepped inside, shaking with joy. He told Good Will all he had been through since leaving home. When he spoke about the hill of fire, Good Will said, "That mountain has been the death of many, and will be the death of many more. It's well you escaped being dashed to pieces."

"I don't know what might have happened to me there," Christian said, "if Evangelist hadn't met me again, by God's mercy. But now here I've come, such as I am. I know I deserve dying more than I deserve standing here talking with you. Oh, what a blessing this is, that I've been let in!"

"We never drive off those who come here," Good Will answered, "no matter what mistakes they made before."

"Now come, and I'll teach you about the way you must go."

TO A CROSS AND A TOMB

OOD WILL pointed ahead. "Look," he said to Christian. "See the narrow path? That's the way you must go, the way built up by the Bible's heroes, and by Christ and his apostles. Other roads run into it which are curvy and wide. That's how you tell a wrong road from the right one: Only the right path is straight and narrow."

He also said Christian would soon come to the house of Interpreter, who would show him excellent things for his journey. So Christian walked onward.

"Come in," said Interpreter afterward, as Christian knocked at his door and explained his journey.

Carrying a candle, Interpreter led Christian inside a dark room. On the wall hung a picture of a man looking up. The best book of all was in his hands, the world was behind his back, and he wore a gold crown.

"What does it mean?" asked Christian.

"This man is one of a thousand," said Interpreter. "The law of truth is written on his lips, and with it he pleads with sinners. His work is to reveal to them deep secrets.

"I showed you this picture first for good reason. The Lord of the place where you're going has chosen this man to be your guide in all the difficulties you meet along your journey. Take good heed to what you see in his picture. Remember him when you meet with someone who tries to trick you into taking the way that leads to death."

Then Interpreter led him into a large room where everything was covered with dust. He called for a servant to come sweep it. But when the man came and swept, so much dust flew about that Christian nearly choked. Interpreter called for another servant, a maiden, who came and first sprinkled the room with water. Then everything was easily cleaned.

"What does this mean?" asked Christian.

"This parlor is a man's heart that was never turned over to God and made holy by the sweet grace of the gospel. The dust is the man's natural sin and the pollution inside him. The first servant who swept is the Law. But the maiden who sprinkled water is the Gospel. The Law stirs up the dirt in our hearts. Only the Gospel can clean a person inside, and make his heart fit for the King to live there."

In the next room were two young children in chairs. One child was called Passion, and the other Patience. Passion was anxious and agitated, while Patience was quiet.

Interpreter explained: "Their teacher promised them good things to come. Passion, however, wants everything now. Patience is willing to wait."

In my dream I saw someone pour out a bag of treasures at Passion's feet. Passion dove into them, and laughed with scorn at Patience. But soon the treasures were all used up, and Passion had nothing left but rags.

"Passion is like those who want all their good things now, in this world," said Interpreter. "The old saying that a bird in the hand is worth two in the bush means more to them than all of God's promises about the age to come. But Patience is like those who are willing to wait for their good things until the next world. And their treasures will never be used up."

In the next room a fire burned up the side of a wall. Someone was there throwing water on it, but the fire only burned higher and hotter.

"What does this mean?" Christian wondered.

Interpreter answered, "The fire is God's work of grace in someone's heart. The one trying to put it out is the devil. And now look."

Interpreter led him behind the burning wall. Someone hidden there was pouring oil on the fire, keeping it going.

"What does this mean?" Christian asked.

"This is Christ," answered Interpreter. "With the oil of his grace he keeps up the work he first began in a person's heart. The hearts of his people stay strong in his grace, no matter what the devil tries to do."

Next Interpreter led him to a beautiful palace. On the roof Christian saw people dressed in gold.

Near the palace entrance Christian saw many men who seemed to want to go in, but dared not. Several armed soldiers stood guard at the doorway. On one side was a man sitting at a table, with a book and pen to write down the names of anyone who would enter the palace.

From fear of the soldiers, all the men but one turned back. But that one stepped boldly up to the table and said, "Sir, write down my name." He drew his sword, put on a helmet, and rushed toward the guards.

They attacked him with deadly force, but the man wasn't at all discouraged. He kept his sword hacking fiercely. After both receiving and giving many wounds, he finally cut his way through the soldiers. He pressed through the door and into the palace, where he was offered golden clothes to wear. Voices sounded inside and from the men on the roof, saying,

Come in, come in!

Eternal glory you will win.

Christian smiled and said, "I think I know what this means. And now I must be on my way."

"No," said Interpreter, "stay till I've showed you a little more."

He led Christian to a dark room. There sat a man in an iron cage. He sighed as if his heart was breaking.

"What does this mean?" Christian asked.

"Talk with him," said Interpreter.

Christian said to the man, "Who are you?"

"I am what I once wasn't," the man answered.

"What were you before?"

"I was a good and growing Christian — at least in my own eyes and the eyes of others. I thought I'd live in the Celestial City, and it made me glad to think so."

"But what are you now?"

"A man shut up in despair, as in this iron cage. I cannot get out. Oh, I cannot get out!"

"But how did you get in?"

"I stopped being careful and alert. I let my feelings and cravings take me wherever they would. I sinned against the goodness of God and the light of his Word. I grieved his Spirit, and now he's gone. I made God angry, and now he's left me. But my heart is hard, and I will not repent."

Christian turned to Interpreter. "Is there any hope for this man?"

"Ask him," said Interpreter.

"No," Christian said. "Please, you ask him."

So Interpreter said, "Must you stay in this cage of despair? Is there no hope?"

"No, none at all," the man answered.

"But the Blessed Son of God is full of mercy and compassion," said Interpreter.

"I'm crucifying him all over again," replied the man. "I hate him. I trample him underfoot and I treat his blood as unholy. I've shut myself off from his promises, and nothing's left for me but threats — dreadful threats, fearful threats of certain judgment and fiery anger, which will eat me up as an enemy. I brought myself here with all my

enjoyments of the world's pleasures and profits. Now all those things bite me and gnaw at me like a burning worm. God himself shut me in this cage, and all the men in the world cannot get me out. Oh, what misery I now must meet for eternity!"

Interpreter said to Christian, "Remember this man, and let his misery be an everlasting warning."

"This is fearful!" Christian replied. "God help me be careful and alert! And now, sir, isn't it time I go on my way?"

"Wait till I show you one thing more," said Interpreter.

He took Christian into a room where a man was getting out of bed. He shook as he put on his robe.

"Tell us why you tremble," Interpreter said.

He answered, "Last night I dreamed the sky blackened, and wind drove the clouds with fury, and there was thunder and lightning. I heard a trumpet, and saw a Man seated on a cloud, with thousands of fiery angels. A voice commanded, 'Arise, you who are dead, and be judged!' Rocks ripped apart, and graves opened, and the dead came out. Some were glad and looked up. Others tried to hide beneath the mountains.

"Then the Man on the cloud opened a book, and ordered the world to draw near. He shouted, 'Throw all the weeds and chaff and stubble into the burning lake!' A bottomless pit opened up near my feet. Smoke and fire and hideous noises came out of it.

"Then the Man shouted, 'Gather my wheat into my barn.' I saw many people carried up into the clouds, while I was left behind. But the Man kept his eye on me, and his look was not pleasant. I tried to hide. Then I woke up."

Interpreter led Christian away. "Have you considered all these things?" he said.

"Yes," Christian answered, "and they give me both hope and fear."

Interpreter nodded. "The Comforter be with you always, good Christian, to guide you in the way that leads to the City."

Now at last Christian went on his way, singing with thankfulness for all he had seen at Interpreter's house. And I saw in my dream that his road sloped up and was bordered on either side by a wall called Salvation. Christian ran up the way, but it was hard because of the load on his back. He ran till he came to a higher place, and on it stood a cross. Down below the rise was a tomb like a cave.

So I saw in my dream that just as Christian came near the cross, his burden slipped from his shoulders and fell from his back. Down the rise it tumbled over and over, till it disappeared into the mouth of the tomb. And I saw it no more.

The Hill Difficulty

CHRISTIAN STOOD THERE awhile to look in wonder at the cross. He was surprised that the simple sight of it should free him from his burden. With a glad heart he said, "By the Lord's sorrow he has given me rest; by his death he's given me life." So he looked and looked again, until tears streamed down his cheeks.

Three Shining Ones then came and greeted him with the words, "Peace to you!"

"Your sins are forgiven," the first Shining One said.

The second took away Christian's rags and gave him rich clothing to wear.

The third marked Christian with a seal on his forehead, and gave him a scroll. "Look upon it as you run," he said, "then return it when you reach the Celestial Gate."

As the Shining Ones left him, Christian gave three leaps for joy, then went on his way singing. Down the path he soon saw three men asleep to one side, with chains on their ankles. One was named Simple, another Sloth, and the third Presumption.

Christian rushed over to them and shouted, "Wake up and come away! You're like someone sleeping at the top of a ship's mast, and there's a Dead Sea under you, an ocean that has no bottom. Wake up!"

They looked at him. "I see no danger," said Simple. "Just a little more sleep," said Sloth. Presumption added, "Each pot must sit on its own bottom, and that's all I can say." They all rolled over to sleep again.

Christian went on, troubled that they should think so little of his offer to help.

Further on he saw two men tumble over a wall and enter the path. The name of one was Formalist, and the other Hypocrisy.

"Where are you from?" Christian asked. "And where are you going?"

"We were born in the land of Vainglory," they answered, "and we go for praise to Mount Zion."

"Why didn't you come in at the gate? Don't you know that it's written, 'The man who doesn't enter by the gate, but climbs in some other way, is a thief and a robber'?"

"We took a short cut, as we usually do," the men answered. "Besides, what does it matter which way we entered? If we're in, we're in."

"But you've violated the rules of the Lord of the Celestial City. Won't that be charged against you?"

"Mind your own business," they said. "Besides, we look the same as you, except for those clothes you wear, which must have been given to you by some neighbor to hide your shameful nakedness."

"The clothes on my back are from the Lord of the place I go," Christian replied. "And yes, they were given to cover my nakedness. I take them as a token of his kindness, for I had nothing but rags before. When I reach the city the Lord will surely know me, since I wear his garments, and I bear his mark on my forehead, and I carry his scroll as my comfort along the way and my passport to enter the city. All these things you don't have, because you didn't come in at the gate. You entered outside God's directions, and I doubt you'll be saved in the end."

They only laughed at him. All of them continued on, but Christian stayed ahead of the others, and talked only with himself. Sometimes he sighed, and sometimes he spoke words of comfort. He read often in the scroll, which always refreshed him.

When he reached the foot of the Hill Difficulty, he saw a spring. The narrow path went straight up the hill, but two other paths went around it, one to the left and one to the right. One was named Danger, and the other Destruction.

Christian took a refreshing drink from the spring, then took a running start up the hill.

The other two also approached. But one took the path called Danger, which took him into an enormous forest. The other man took the path called Destruction. It led into a wide field full of mounds, which made the man stumble and fall, and he never got up.

High on the Hill Difficulty I saw Christian slow his pace from running to walking, and from walking to climbing on hands and knees, because of the steepness. Midway to the top was a shady spot, a place made by the Lord of the hill for weary travelers to stop a moment and rest. There Christian sat down and opened his scroll to read for his comfort. He also looked closer at his new clothes.

Pleased with himself, he grew drowsy, and finally went fast asleep. The daylight began fading, and while he slept, his scroll slipped from his hand.

Then he heard someone saying, "Go to the ant, you sluggard! Consider its ways and be wise!" Christian was startled awake. He rose and hurried onward, up the hill.

Near the top, two men came running toward him. One was named Timid, and the other Mistrust.

"Sirs, you're running the wrong way," Christian said.

"We're going back," said Timid. "This path becomes too dangerous!"

"Yes," said Mistrust. "We saw two lions, and we knew they would attack if we got closer." On they ran, back down the hill.

Their words made Christian afraid, but he kept going. He knew he could never go back to his own city for safety, since it was to be destroyed by fire. Wanting comfort, Christian decided to read his scroll. To his great distress he discovered he no longer had it. He remembered reading it at the shady place — but then and there he had fallen asleep.

Now he fell to his knees and asked God's forgiveness for that foolish mistake. With great sorrow he turned back to find the scroll. With every step he searched both sides of the path. He sighed, and wept, and scolded himself for being so foolish.

Finally he saw the shady spot ahead, but the sight only deepened his sorrow for his mistake. "O wretched man that I am," he said, "to sleep during the day, and choose comfort in the time for difficulty!"

He cried again when he reached the shady spot. There he saw the scroll. He grabbed it and held it close, then again took up his journey. For the third time he covered the same stretch of ground that he should have walked over only once.

The sun went down. Remembering what Mistrust and Timid had said about the lions, and knowing these beasts hunt at night, Christian wondered how he would escape being torn to pieces.

THE PALACE BEAUTIFUL

UT WHILE HE MOANED his misfortune, Christian lifted his eyes. Before him he saw a stately palace called Beautiful.

In my dream I saw Christian hurry into a narrow passageway that led a good distance to a gatekeeper's post. But closer to him, Christian saw two lions.

He now considered going after Mistrust and Timid. But the gatekeeper, named Watchful, saw Christian hesitate. He called out, "Is your strength so small? Don't fear the lions; they're chained. They're a test of faith, to separate those who have it from those who don't. Stay in the middle of the path, and no harm will come to you."

Christian stepped forward, trembling with fear, and taking heed to the gatekeeper's directions. He heard the lions roar, but they did not hurt him. He clapped his hands for joy when he came to the gatekeeper. "Sir, what house is this, and may I lodge here tonight?"

Watchful answered, "The house was built by the Lord of the hill for the rest and safety of pilgrims. Where are you from, and where are you going?"

"I come from the City of Destruction, and I go to Mount Zion."

"What is your name?"

"My name is Christian."

"Why have you come here so late? The sun's already set."

Christian explained about his falling asleep.

"I'll call one of the ladies of this place," said Watchful. He rang a bell. Out the palace door stepped a beautiful woman whose name was Discretion.

"This man asked if he might lodge here tonight," Watchful told her.

Discretion asked Christian where he was from, and where he was going, and he told her. She asked how he entered the path, and he told her. She asked what he had seen and met along the way, and he told her. Then she asked his name.

"Christian," he answered, "and now I want to stay here tonight even more, knowing that this place was built for pilgrims by the Lord of the hill."

Discretion smiled, and tears were in her eyes. She called out her sisters Prudence, Piety, and Charity, and they said to him, "Come in, you who are blessed by the Lord."

Inside, as supper was being prepared, they gave him something to drink and they talked with him. "What made you choose to become a pilgrim?" asked Piety.

Christian told about his fear of the coming destruction if he stayed in his city, and how Evangelist showed him the way out.

Then Prudence asked, "Do you still think about the country you left behind?"

"Yes," Christian answered, "but now I desire a better country, a heavenly one."

"Do you still sometimes have worldly thoughts?" Prudence asked.

"Yes, but against my will. If I could, I'd never think of those things again."

"Do you sometimes find victory over those worldly thoughts?"

"Yes," said Christian, "and those rare times are golden hours to me."

"And in those times, how do you find this victory?"

"When I think about what I saw at the cross, and what happened to me there, that will do it. And when I look into the scroll I carry, that will do it. And when I think about where I'm going, that will do it too."

"What makes you want to go to Mount Zion?" Prudence asked.

"I hope to see alive there the One who hung dead on the cross. To tell you the truth, I love him, because he took away my burden. I also hope there to get rid of all my inward worldliness, because I'm weary of it. And I want to be there in the good company of those who always say, 'Holy, holy, holy!'"

Then her sister Charity asked Christian, "Do you have a family?"

"Yes, a wife and four small children."

"Why didn't you bring them with you?"

Christian wept. "Oh, how I tried," he said, "but they didn't even want me to come."

"You should have talked with them and shown them their danger," said Charity.

"I did. I told them everything. But they didn't believe me."

"Did you pray that God would bless your words to them?"

"Yes, deeply. For my wife and poor children are very dear to me."

"Did you tell them of your own sorrow and fear of destruction?"

"Yes, over and over and over, and with tears and trembling. But my wife was afraid of losing this world. And my children wanted only the foolish delights of youth."

Now I saw in my dream that their supper was ready, and they all sat down to eat and drink a fine meal. Their talk at the table was about the Lord of the hill, and all he had done, and why he had built this palace. They mentioned that he was a great warrior, and had fought and destroyed the one who held the power of death.

"And I love him even more," said Christian, "because he did this with the loss of much blood, out of pure love for the world, and for poor pilgrims."

They mentioned also how the Lord had caused many pilgrims to become princes.

They talked together like this until late at night. Then they prayed and asked for the Lord's protection, and went to bed. They led Christian to a large upper bedroom with a window opening toward the rising of the sun. And the name of his room was Peace.

A FIGHT WITH APOLLYON

HRISTIAN SLEPT till the break of day. As he woke, he wondered, *Where am I now?* When he remembered he was in the Palace Beautiful, he treasured the thought of how Jesus loves and cares for pilgrims. "He forgave me," Christian sang, "and now he lets me live next-door to heaven!"

Soon everyone was up. The sisters took Christian to see the rare riches of the palace. In the library they read to him from books that were older than old. The books told about the Lord of the hill, the Son of One who was called the Ancient of Days, and had lived forever. They showed great deeds the Lord had done, and gave the names of hundreds whom he chose to be his servants, and explained how he gave them homes to last forever.

The books also told how these servants conquered kingdoms, and shut the mouth of lions, and smothered fiery explosions, and escaped the edge of the sword. They were strong even in their weakness, and became heroes in battle, and made enemy armies surrender.

Another book told how ready the Lord is to be anyone's friend, no matter how much that person has insulted or hated him before. In other books there were famous stories new and old that Christian had heard. More books told what would happen in the future — things to surprise and frighten the Lord's enemies, and bring comfort and relief to pilgrims.

The next day the sisters showed Christian the armory. It held enough equipment to outfit as many soldiers of the Lord as there are stars in heaven. They showed him all kinds of armor: sword and shield, helmet and breastplate, a piece called all-prayer, and battle-shoes that could not wear out.

In another chamber they showed him the staff Moses had carried, and the jars and trumpets and torches Gideon used to turn back the armies of Midian. Christian saw the donkey's jawbone with which Samson killed a thousand Philistines, and the sling and stone David used to kill Goliath. Christian was delighted to see them all, and many other excellent things that day, before everyone rested again.

Then I saw in my dream that two mornings later, when the weather was clear, the sisters climbed with Christian to the top of the palace, to show him the Delectable Mountains. "Seeing them will make you glad," they said, "because they're closer to your journey's end than where you are now."

When they reached the top, they said, "Look south." Christian did. Far away he saw mountains covered with woods and grapevines and fruit trees and flowers, and flowing with springs and fountains. He asked the name of that country.

"It's called Immanuel's Land," they said. "When you arrive there, shepherds will show you the gate to the Celestial City."

Now Christian felt it was time to set out again on his journey. "But first," the sisters said, "let's return to the armory."

There they fitted him out with proven armor all over, then went with him to the palace gate. Christian said to Watchful, the gatekeeper, "Have any other pilgrims passed by?"

"One," Watchful answered. "I asked his name, and he said, 'Faithful.'"

"I know him!" Christian exclaimed. "He's my neighbor from the town where I was born. How far ahead do you think he may be?"

"Below the hill by now," said Watchful.

The sisters began walking down the hill with Christian, who said, "I can see that just as it was difficult getting here, it will be dangerous going onward."

"Yes," answered Prudence. "It's hard for anyone not to trip and fall going down into the Valley of Humility, as you are now. We'll walk with you, as far as the foot of the hill."

Christian carefully made his way down, but still he slipped twice.

Then I saw in my dream that at the bottom of the hill, these good friends gave Christian bread and wine and raisins. Then he went on alone into the Valley of Humility.

He hadn't gone far when a monster came across a field toward him. His name was Apollyon. In fear, Christian wondered if he should turn and run. When he remembered he had no armor covering his back, where the monster's darts could easily wound him, he decided to stand his ground.

The monster looked hideous. The fishlike scales that covered him were his pride. He had wings like a dragon, feet like a bear, and a mouth like a lion. Out of his belly came

fire and smoke. He looked down on Christian and sneered, "Where do you come from? And where are you bound?"

Christian answered, "I'm from the City of Destruction, a place of evil. And I go to the City of Zion."

Apollyon roared, "Then you're one of my subjects, for the country you left belongs to me. I am the prince and god of it. Why have you run away from my rule? If I didn't have plans for you, I would strike you to the ground with one blow."

"Indeed," said Christian, "I was born into your kingdom. But serving you was hard, and no one could live on what you pay, for the wages of sin is death. When I grew older, I did what any sensible person would do: I looked for something better."

"No prince lets go of his subject so easily," Apollyon snarled. "Nor will I release you. But since you complain of the work and the pay, return now, and I promise to give you whatever my country can afford."

"But I've given myself to Someone else," Christian answered. "I belong to the King of kings. So in fairness, how could I go back with you?"

"Those who take up with this King of yours usually drop him after a while," replied Apollyon, "and come back to me. If you do the same, all will be well."

"But I promised to follow him faithfully! How could I turn my back on him, and not be punished as a traitor?"

"But first you belonged to *me*, and turned your back on *me*," Apollyon said smoothly. "Yet I'm willing to overlook it, if you'll return."

"I belonged to you when I was too young to know better," Christian declared. "I know my King will forgive me for all the wrong I did in serving you. Besides, you destroyer — to tell the truth, I like his service and his pay and his servants and his country better than yours. So stop trying to win me back. I am his servant, and I will follow him."

"Cool off," responded Apollyon. "Just think what's ahead on the road you've chosen. Those who serve that King always find trouble. Oh, how many of them have been put to a shameful death! And he never comes to save them. But I'm always saving *my* servants out of his power. I'll do the same for you."

Christian quickly answered, "The King waits to save his servants only to let them first prove their love. If they stay faithful to him in all their troubles, he will reward them in the end, when he comes in his glory and the glory of his angels."

"Ahh," spoke Apollyon, "but you've already been unfaithful to him! How can you expect to get any reward?"

"When?" cried Christian. "When was I unfaithful to him?"

"You've stumbled ever since you set out," Apollyon answered boldly. "You fell into the Slough of Despond. You tried to get rid of your burden the wrong way instead of letting the King do it. You slept when you were supposed to be awake, and while you slept you lost what you were supposed to keep. When you saw lions you almost turned back. Furthermore, when you talk about your dangerous journey, down deep you're all proud about it, and you want everyone to notice you."

Christian sighed, and answered, "All this is true, and much more that you've left out. But the King I serve and honor is merciful, and ready to forgive. Besides, all those weaknesses first came to me in *your* country, where I sucked them in. I've groaned about them, and I've been sorry for them, and my King has forgiven me."

Now Apollyon broke into a terrible rage. "I am an enemy to this King! I hate him and his laws and his people! And I have come out on purpose to fight you!"

"Beware, Apollyon!" Christian shouted. "I'm on the King's highway, the way of holiness. Therefore take heed!"

Apollyon threw himself across the road. "I'm not afraid," he bellowed. "Prepare to die, for I swear by my house of fire that you'll go no further. Right here I will spill your soul!"

He threw a flaming dart at Christian's chest, but it caught in his shield.

Christian drew his sword just as Apollyon began throwing darts as thick as hail. They struck him in the face and hands and feet. Wounded, he began to step back. Apollyon at once came closer, but Christian again took courage, and resisted as manfully as he could.

The combat went on more than half a day. Hideous roars came all the while from Apollyon's throat. Christian groaned, and grew weaker and weaker.

Finally, seeing his opportunity, Apollyon flung himself upon Christian to wrestle him. Christian's sword flew from his hand.

"I have you now!" Apollyon yelled. He pressed his weight down on the pilgrim. Christian began to despair of life. But as God would have it, while Apollyon prepared to strike the last blow, Christian's outstretched fingers touched his sword. He gripped it. With all his might, he gave the beast one deadly thrust.

In pain Apollyon jerked out his wings and flew violently away.

For the first time that day, Christian smiled. Still on the ground with his wounds, he said, "In all these things we are more than conquerors through him who loves us." Then he looked up and gave thanks to the One who had delivered him.

And so, for a season, he saw Apollyon no more.

The Valley of
the Shadow of Death

N MY DREAM I saw a hand reach down, holding leaves from the tree of life. Christian touched them to his battle wounds, which were healed at once.

He stayed there to eat bread and drink the wine he had been given. Being refreshed, he gave himself again to his journey, with his sword drawn in his hand.

At the end of that valley was another, called the Valley of the Shadow of Death. It was barren wilderness, a land of deserts and canyons, a land of dryness and darkness, where no one lived.

Where the valley began, Christian met two men coming quickly from the other direction.

"Where are you going?" he asked.

"Back! Back!" they said. "And so should you, if you value life or peace."

"Why? What's the matter?"

"The valley's dark as pitch," they answered. "We saw hobgoblins and monsters and pit-dragons. We heard howling and yelling, like people crying out in torture. Clouds of confusion hung over the valley, and death's wings were spread over it. It's all dreadful. We went only as far as we dared!"

"From all you say," answered Christian, "this is the way to the heaven I desire."

"Not for us," said the men, and they left him. Christian continued with his drawn sword still in his hand. Nightfall had come again.

I saw in my dream that all along the path through the valley was a deep trench on the right, where the blind lead the blind and all of them perish. On the left was a quagmire of quicksand. Even a good man who fell in would find no bottom for his foot to stand on.

The pathway was more narrow than before. I sensed also that somewhere ahead was the mouth of hell, right beside the path.

It was now so dark that Christian could not see one step ahead. He struggled to avoid the trench on one side and the quagmire on the other. I heard him sigh bitterly.

Here and there flames and smoke would burst up, with crackling sparks and other hideous noises. Christian knew his sword was useless against such things. He put it away and pulled out the weapon called all-prayer. "O Lord," Christian cried, "save me!"

Still the flames jumped out at him.

For miles he made his way forward. Voices somewhere were crying in agony. He also heard things rushing here and there, and imagined himself being trampled or torn by whatever they were.

At one place he was sure he heard a gang of evil spirits approaching. He considered turning back, but he hoped the dangers ahead might be less than those he'd already passed. He resolved to keep going.

The demons seemed to get closer and closer. Finally, when he sensed they were almost upon him, he cried out as loudly as he could, "I will walk in the strength of the Lord God!" The evil spirits drew back.

I noticed now that as Christian passed the mouth of hell, a wicked one stepped up softly behind him. Into Christian's ear he whispered many curses and hateful things against the God whom Christian loved. Christian was in such confusion that he thought it was his own voice saying these horrible lies, and he didn't know to stop his ears.

Further on, Christian thought he heard a man's voice ahead. The man was praying these words: "Though I walk through the valley of the shadow of death, I will fear no evil, for you are with me." Christian was overjoyed that someone else who worshiped God was there in this valley. And he thought, *If God is with this man in such a dark and dismal place, surely he'll also be with me.* Hoping to catch up with the man, Christian called out to him, but heard no answer.

Finally he saw daylight coming on. "The Lord has turned my darkness into dawn," he said. He looked back where he'd been. In the morning light he saw more clearly the trench and the quagmire, and the narrow path, and the hobgoblins and monsters and pit-dragons.

Then Christian looked forward. By the light of the rising sun he saw that the part of the valley still ahead of him was even worse than where he'd been. He saw snares and traps and nets. The valley floor was full of pits and deep holes and hollows and slippery slopes. If he had to cross it in darkness, Christian knew he would never make it, even if he had a thousand lives. He thanked God for the lamp of his sunlight.

In this light he went on. And in this light he finally reached the end of the valley.

Now I saw in my dream that Christian passed a pile of bones, ashes, and mangled

bodies — all that was left of some men who went this way before. Two giants living in a cave nearby had killed those pilgrims. But the giant named Pagan was dead, and the one named Pompous was now an old man, crazy and stiff. He sat at the mouth of the cave, staring at pilgrims going by and biting his nails because he couldn't come after them. He shouted at Christian, "More of you will be burned!" But Christian went by without harm.

He came to a place where the path was on a clear hilltop. Ahead of him he saw his neighbor Faithful from the City of Destruction. "Ho!" Christian shouted. "Stay and I'll come walk with you!"

Faithful looked back and cried, "No, I can't stop. There's danger behind me."

Christian used all his strength to catch up with Faithful, and then ran on ahead of him. He looked back with a proud smile at being faster than Faithful. But not being careful, he suddenly stumbled and fell. He couldn't get up until Faithful came and helped him.

Then the two men gladly walked and talked together. Faithful said he left home soon after Christian did, because he was convinced their city would soon be destroyed with fire from above. They each told one another about the dangers and deliverances they had met so far.

Faithful had not fallen into the Slough of Despond, but later he met someone named

Loose Woman. She flattered him with her words, and promised him every kind of happiness. But Faithful remembered the Scripture that says, "Her feet go down to death, her steps take hold of hell." He shut his eyes so he wouldn't see her bewitching looks. She yelled at him, but he went on his way.

Faithful came to the Palace Beautiful in the middle of the day, when the lions were sleeping. He had greeted the gatekeeper and continued on. In the Valley of Humility he met a man named Discontent, who told Faithful that if he didn't turn back, it would upset his friends, who were named Pride, Arrogance, Self-Conceit, and Worldly-Glory.

"How did you answer him?" Christian said.

"I told him that the people he named were once my friends and brothers by the flesh. But now I rejected them, and wanted nothing more to do with them."

Faithful said he then met a man named Shame who was the hardest person of all to get away from.

"What did he say?" Christian asked.

"He said that living for God was a pitiful, low, sneaking business for anyone to be part of. He said it isn't manly to think about God and to be careful how you live. He said people who are powerful or rich or smart would have nothing to do with it. He said pilgrims are always poor and ignorant and weak. He said it's a *shame* for anyone to think and cry about what's written in the Bible. He said it's a *shame* for anyone to ask for a neighbor's forgiveness."

"And how did you answer him?"

"At first I couldn't think what to say. Then I told him that what men see as treasure, God sees as worthless. I said, 'Shame, you tell me what men say, but not what God says. And what God says is best, even if every man in the world was against it.'

"Then I said, 'Shame, get away from me! You're an enemy to my salvation.' But Shame was a bold rascal, and kept haunting me and whispering in my ear. At last I told him it was useless to keep nagging me, because the things he hated were the things I loved. So at last I shook him off, and then I began to sing."

"I'm glad you handled him so bravely," said Christian. "Let's resist him the same if we meet him again."

"Yes," replied Faithful, "and cry out for God's help against him."

A Talker Comes and Goes

HERE THE PATH grew wider, I saw in my dream that Faithful looked to one side and saw another traveler. He was a tall man, and handsome from a distance.

"Friend!" Faithful called to the traveler. "Are you going to the heavenly country?"

"I am," he replied.

"Good!" said Faithful. "I hope we may have your good company. Come walk with us, and we'll talk about things that really matter."

"I'll gladly be your companion," the man said. "I like talking about important topics, with you or with anyone. For instance, I like to talk about the history and the mystery of things, and about miracles and wonders and signs. It's profitable to discuss such matters, for by it a man can gain much knowledge."

"So," said Faithful as the man came close, "what shall we talk about?"

"Oh, whatever," the man answered. "I'll talk about things heavenly or things earthly, things holy or things unholy, things past or things to come, things faraway or things nearby, things big or things little. I'll talk about anything, as long as it's profitable."

Faithful was in awe of this traveler, and he stepped aside and whispered to Christian, "What a brave companion we've got. Surely this man will make an excellent pilgrim!"

Christian smiled. "This man who so impresses you will fool you with his tongue, as many can tell you."

"Do you know him?" Faithful asked.

"Yes. Better than he knows himself. His name is Talkative. He lives in our city, and I'm surprised you never met him. He's the son of Mr. Say-Well, and his house is on Babbling Lane. He has a skillful tongue but he's a sorry fellow."

"But he looks fine," said Faithful.

"That he does," Christian replied, "to those who don't know him. But he's ugly enough at home, where he always insults his poor family. And his neighbors say he's a cheat and a liar."

"He certainly fooled me."

"That he did," said Christian. "Out traveling he'll talk with anyone as he did with you. He especially talks in taverns, after he fills his head with drink. He chatters about prayer and repentance and faith and being born again. But it's all talk, all lies. There's no truth of it in his heart or in his home or in his behavior."

"Now I see," said Faithful, "that saying and doing are two different things. I'll start looking closer for the difference. But how do we get rid of this man?"

"I have an idea," said Christian. "Ask him about the change God's grace can bring to a person's life. After he's babbled about it (which he surely will), ask him if he's seen such a change in his own heart and home and behavior. He'll soon grow sick of our company, unless God changes him."

So Faithful stepped over and said to Talkative, "Here's a question for you: When God's grace is in a person's heart, what difference does it make?"

"Good question," Talkative answered. "And my answer goes like this. First, when God's grace is in a man's heart, it causes him to speak out against sin. Second—"

"Wait!" said Faithful. "Shouldn't you say instead that it makes a man *hate* sin?"

"Why, what difference is there between speaking out against sin and hating it?"

"Oh, a great deal. Some men speak out against sin, but they let it stay in their home and their hearts and their behavior."

"I think you're trying to trick me," said Talkative.

"No, not me. I just like to set things out right. Now what's your second point?"

"My second point is that when God's grace is in a man's heart, he gains great knowledge of gospel mysteries."

"That's not true," said Faithful. "A man can gain great knowledge *without* God's grace. A man can have all knowledge, and yet be nothing. When Jesus asked his disciples, 'Do you *know* these things,' he then said, 'You will be blessed if you *do* them.' The blessing comes from *doing*, not knowing. Just knowing something is fine with talkers and boasters. But it takes *doing* to please God."

"You're trying to trick me again," said Talkative. "And I won't say anymore."

"Then allow me to, if you will," Faithful said. "When God's grace is working within someone, it shows him his sin. And it makes him sorry and shameful for it. It shows him the Savior of the world, and how absolutely necessary it is to believe in him. It makes a man hungry and thirsty to follow him. And the more he believes in the Savior the more joy and peace he knows, and the more he longs to be like the Savior in his heart and in his home and in his behavior.

"So tell me, sir, have you experienced all this? Or is your religion only talk?"

Talkative's face turned red. "I didn't expect this kind of discussion," he said.

And he walked away.

Christian and Faithful now entered a wilderness. But they had one another to make the going pleasant instead of tiresome. When they were close to leaving the wilderness, Faithful happened to look back and see someone coming up to them. It was Evangelist, who had been a good friend and guide to Faithful as well as to Christian. Both men welcomed him and told him of the difficulties they had faced since they last saw him.

Evangelist answered, "How glad I am — not that you met trials and dangers, but that you were victors over them, and are still on the path today. A crown awaits you, a crown that will last forever. Hold on to what you have, so no one will take away your crown. You're not yet out of the devil's gunshot, so keep the kingdom always before you, and never stop believing the things that are invisible. Above all else guard your hearts, for they are deceitful and desperately wicked. Set your faces like flint. You have all power in heaven and earth on your side."

Christian thanked him for his words, and added, "Since we know you're a prophet, and can tell what might happen to us on the rest of our journey, what further help can you give us?"

Evangelist answered, "You must go through many trials to enter the kingdom of heaven. You can't expect to go far without meeting afflictions. You've known some already, and more will follow. You're almost out of this wilderness, and soon you'll come to a town where you'll face many enemies. One or both of you will be required there to seal your testimony with your blood. But be faithful unto death, and the King will give you a crown of life."

VANITY FAIR

HEN I SAW in my dream that the pilgrims left the wilderness and saw the town before them. The name of it is Vanity, because everything there is empty and vain.

A fair is held there all year long. Its name is Vanity Fair, because everything sold or shown there is hollow and worthless. All kinds of merchandise are displayed: houses and land, honors and awards, countries and kingdoms, and all sorts of pleasures and delights. There are bodies and blood, and souls and silver and gold, and pearls and precious stones. At any time there you find all kinds of jugglers and cheats and tricksters and fools and apes and rascals. For free you can see robberies and murders and lies, all as red as blood.

The fair is ancient. It was set up five thousand years ago by Beelzebub the devil and his companions.

The way to the Celestial City passes through this town. So the pilgrims entered it. They made quite a stir walking along. Their clothes were not like those bought at the fair. And their speech sounded strange, for Christian and Faithful spoke the language of the Promised Land. So people stared at them, calling them fools or idiots or show-offs.

The merchants at the fair were especially upset because Christian and Faithful didn't listen when the merchants urged them to buy. The pilgrims put their fingers in their ears and looked up and prayed, "Turn my eyes away from worthless things."

"What *will* you buy?" one merchant asked.

"We buy the truth," the pilgrims answered.

This made the merchants despise them even more. They mocked and insulted the pilgrims. Then someone shouted, "Beat them!"

So things came to an uproar, and because of the confusion, Faithful and Christian were arrested and taken before the city authorities. "Where are you from?" they asked, "and where are you going, and why do you wear such strange clothing?"

They answered that they were pilgrims and strangers in this world, they were going to their own country, the heavenly Jerusalem, and there was no reason for merchants at the fair to treat them roughly.

The authorities decided Faithful and Christian were foolish troublemakers. They were beaten, smeared all over with dirt, and put in a cage for everyone to see. People rudely laughed and jeered at them. But Faithful and Christian were patient and said nothing rude in return. Instead they blessed the people, speaking kind and good words to them.

That made a few people begin speaking out against the rougher folks who insulted the pilgrims. "You're worse than the men in the cage!" they said. So the people argued among themselves, and soon they were fighting each other, and that got the attention of the authorities again.

Faithful and Christian were charged with causing another disturbance. They were beaten once more. They were chained in irons and dragged up and down the streets. The pilgrims still behaved with meekness and patience, but this only enraged many of the people. Someone shouted that the two men should die.

They were thrown in the cage again. They remembered now what Evangelist had said. They comforted one another, and agreed that if one of them was to suffer and die, that man would have the best of it. Each one secretly hoped he himself would be the one killed, but they trusted God's wisdom to decide.

Now they were brought to trial before a judge named Lord Hate-Good, and a jury of twelve men. Their names were Mr. Blind-Man, Mr. No-Good, Mr. Malice, Mr. Love-Lust, Mr. Live-Loose, Mr. Heady, Mr. High-Mind, Mr. Enmity, Mr. Liar, Mr. Cruelty, Mr. Hate-Light, and Mr. Rigid.

Faithful and Christian were charged with disturbing business at the fair, causing commotion and disunity in the town, and not respecting the law of the city's prince.

Faithful answered the charge first. He said he was a man of peace, and that the disturbance and commotion were caused by others. "And as for the prince you talk of," he added, "since he is the devil Beelzebub, the enemy of our Lord, I defy him and all his demons!"

Three witnesses came in to speak against the pilgrims. Their names were Envy, Superstition, and Pickthank.

Envy stood first. Pointing to Faithful, he said, "I've known this man a long time, and he's one of the worst in our country. He's a traitor, and he does all he can to fill others with his disloyal ideas, which he calls faith and holiness. I myself once heard him say his Christianity is an enemy to the way we do things in the town of Vanity. So he hates not only the wonderful things we do, but us as well."

Then they called Superstition to speak. He looked at Faithful and said, "I don't know this man, nor do I ever want to. But I do know he's a pest. The other day I heard him say our religion in this town isn't pleasing to God. That's just like saying our worship is empty, and that we're still in our sins and will be sent to hell."

Now it was Pickthank's turn to go against Faithful.

"I've known this fellow a long while, and I've heard him speak what should never be spoken. He railed against our noble prince Beelzebub, and he talked against our prince's honorable friends, including Lord Old Man, Lord Carnal Delight, Lord Luxurious, Lord Desire of Vain Glory, Lord Lust, and Sir Having Greed, plus all the rest of our nobility. He said if he had his way, no one in this town would belong to these noblemen. Besides this, he also spoke against you, Lord Hate-Good. He called you an ungodly villain."

The judge looked at Faithful and said, "You outlaw and heretic and traitor, have you heard what these honest gentlemen have witnessed against you?"

"May I speak a few words in my defense?" Faithful asked.

"Sir!" answered the judge. "You deserve only death at once. But just so everyone can see how kind we are toward you, let's hear what you have to say, you outlaw!"

So Faithful stood. "In answer to what Mr. Envy has spoken, what I have said is this: Any custom or rule or law that's against God's Word will also be an enemy to Christianity.

"In answer to Mr. Superstition, what I have said is this: True worship that pleases God comes only from the faith that's taught in the Scriptures.

"And in answer to Mr. Pickthank, what I say is this: The prince of this town and all his noble friends are more fit to stay in hell than in this town and country."

Lord Hate-Good told the jury the case against Faithful was now theirs to decide. "It lies in your hands to either hang him or save him," he said.

The twelve men talked together to make their decision. They quickly found Faithful guilty. "I see clearly this man is a heretic," said Blind-Man. "I hate the very looks of him," said Malice. "Away with such a fellow from the earth," said No-Good. "A sorry scrub," said High-Mind. "Hang him! Hang him!" said Heady. "Hanging is too good for him," said Cruelty.

So they brought him out and whipped him, then beat him, then cut him with knives, then stoned him with stones, then pricked him with swords. Last of all they burned him to ashes. So Faithful came to his end.

But now above all the crowd I saw a chariot and horses waiting. As a trumpet sounded they caught up Faithful and carried him away, straight through the clouds — the shortest way to the Celestial Gate.

Christian, meanwhile, was taken back to prison.

A New Friend, and New Enemies

HRISTIAN REMAINED in prison awhile. Then God, who has power over all things, worked it out for him to escape. Christian went on his way with this song:

Sing, Faithful, sing, and let your name survive;
for though they killed you, you are yet alive.

But Christian did not have to keep walking alone. A man whose new name was Hopeful had witnessed the words and behavior and sufferings of Faithful and Christian in the town of Vanity, and now he left that town to find Christian. He joined in a bond of brotherhood with him, and they agreed to journey together.

And so one man died bearing testimony to the truth, while out of his ashes another man rose to take his place at Christian's side.

Not far from Vanity they caught up with yet another man. He didn't tell them his name, but said he was from the town of Fair-Speech.

"I've heard about this town," said Christian. "They say it's a wealthy place."

"It is for sure," the man said. "I come from a rich family myself. My great-grandfather made his money in a boat, looking one way and rowing another. That's how I earned most of my money too.

"All my relatives are good quality," he continued. "It's true we're not exactly like people who are more strict in their faith, but we're different only in two small points. First, we never go against wind and tide. And second, we're always most committed to our religion when religion wears silver slippers. We love to walk with religion in the street when the sun shines, and the people applaud."

"I'm thinking now I recall who you are," said Christian. "Isn't your name Mr. Get-Gain?"

"No it isn't. That's just a nickname put upon me by people who don't like me."

"But you must have given them some reason to call you that."

"Never," replied Get-Gain. "The worst I ever did was to be lucky enough to make money by jumping in at the right place and the right time. I count that a blessing, no matter what people call me.

"Now may I walk with you on your journey to the Celestial City?"

"If you go with us," said Christian, "you must go against wind and tide. You must follow the way of faith whether it means rags or silver slippers, whether rain or sunshine, and whether prison or applause."

At that, Get-Gain dropped back from walking with Christian and Hopeful. But soon he returned with three friends — Money-Love, Hold-the-World, and Save-All. They had a question for Christian and Hopeful.

"Answer if you can," they said. "Suppose a man has the chance to get a lot of money and good things, but it so happens the only way he can get them is to appear very faithful and religious, even though he didn't meddle in those things before. Isn't it right for him to go ahead and do this, and isn't he still an honest man if he does?"

Christian answered, "It's something God hates, when anyone tries to use the way of faith as a means to make money. The only people who do such a thing are pagans and hypocrites and devils and witches."

Get-Gain and his friends could say nothing in reply. They staggered back away.

Then Christian and Hopeful came to a little hill called Wealth. On it there was a silver mine. Many pilgrims before had left the path to go see it. But because the land around the mine was unstable, the ground often broke open beneath their feet, and they were killed or terribly hurt.

I saw in my dream that beside the silver mine stood a man named Demas, who was in love with this world. He called out to Christian and Hopeful, "Come here! I'll show you something!"

Hopeful said to Christian, "Let's go see it!"

"No!" replied Christian. He called back to Demas, "Isn't that place dangerous?"

"Not if you're careful," Demas answered.

Christian said to Hopeful, "Let's stick to the path."

But Demas called out again, "Aren't you coming?"

Christian called back, "Demas, you're an enemy to the right ways of the Lord. You've already been condemned for your love of this world. Why should we earn the same punishment?"

Christian and Hopeful went on, but they looked back and saw Get-Gain and his friends drawing near to the hill called Wealth. When Demas called only once, they hurried closer to the silver mine. Suddenly they dropped into a pit, and were never seen again.

Next Christian and Hopeful came to a strange monument. It looked like a statue of

a woman, but it was the color of salt. They saw a sign on it that read, "Remember Lot's wife." This made Hopeful give thanks that he had not been destroyed at the silver mine. "After all," he said, "Lot's wife was turned into a statue of salt only because she looked back at a wicked place far away. But I wanted to go close and see it."

Next they came to a pleasant stream. It was the river King David called the Streams of God, and which John called the River of the Water of Life. Christian and Hopeful walked along its banks with great delight. They drank from the water, which was pleasant and refreshing to their weary spirits. Green trees grew there, bearing all kinds of fruit which they tasted and enjoyed. And the leaves of the trees were good for medicine.

On either side of the river was a meadow, always green, and covered with beautiful flowers. In this meadow they slept, for here they could lie down in safety.

When they awoke, they gathered more fruit and ate it, and drank more water from the river. Then they lay down again to sleep.

And so in this way they passed several days and nights in the meadow, until it was time to take up their journey again. On that last day there they ate once more, and drank, and departed.

THE WRONG WAY

HEY WERE SORRY when their path left the river. I saw in my dream that the ground was rougher here, and their feet grew sore, and their spirits grew discouraged. They wished for a better way.

A little before them, on the left side of the road, was a meadow with a path leading into it. The place is called Bypath Meadow.

Christian and Hopeful took a closer look. "It's just as I wished," Christian said. "This is easier ground. Let's try it."

"But what if it leads us out of the way?" Hopeful asked.

"That isn't likely," Christian answered, "since it goes the same direction." So Hopeful followed Christian, and they both found the new ground easier on their feet.

Down the path they saw a man walking ahead of them. His name was Vain-Confidence. They called out and asked him where this path led to.

"To the Celestial Gate," Vain-Confidence answered.

"See," said Christian to Hopeful. "Didn't I tell you?"

Soon the night came on, and grave darkness. The pilgrims lost sight of the man in front of them. They didn't see him slip and tumble into a deep pit, to be battered by the fall. But they heard the noise of it.

Christian and Hopeful called out, but the only answer was a groaning.

"Where are we?" Hopeful asked.

Christian couldn't answer. He realized now that they were off their rightful path.

It began to rain, with dreadful thunder and lightning. Water rose at their feet.

Hopeful groaned, "Oh, how I wish I'd stayed on the right path!"

"Good brother," Christian said, "I'm sorry I led you astray. I've put you in danger. Please forgive me. I didn't mean any harm from this."

"Brother, be comforted," Hopeful answered. "I forgive you. And I believe this will turn out for our good."

"I'm glad for a merciful brother," said Christian. "And now we can't just stand here. Let's try going back."

The flood waters were growing deeper, and so was the darkness, but the pilgrims kept going. They found a little shelter, and decided to stay there till daybreak, knowing they couldn't reach the right path before morning. Weary, they soon fell asleep.

Not far away was a house called Doubting Castle, whose owner was Giant Despair. The shelter where the pilgrims slept was on his property. When morning came, he was out walking his fields, and found Christian and Hopeful. With a grim and surly voice he woke them up and asked where they were from and why they were trampling and trespassing on his grounds.

They said they were pilgrims and had lost their way.

"Come with me!" he ordered. They had to obey, because he was stronger than they were. He threw them into a dungeon that was dark and filthy and stinking. They were there four days without bread, water, light, or anyone to care for them. Christian had double sorrow, since it was through his wrong advice that they both were there.

Giant Despair had a wife. One night in bed she told her husband he should beat his new prisoners without mercy. The next morning he took a limb from a crabtree and went down to the dungeon. First he yelled at Christian and Hopeful as if they were dogs. Then he beat them as hard as he could, until they lay helpless and still on the dungeon floor.

That night the giant's wife told him he should order his prisoners to kill themselves. The next morning he went to them in the same surly manner as before. He found them in great pain and weakness, hardly able to do anything but breathe. He told them that since they were unlikely ever to leave that place, they should kill themselves with knife or rope or poison. "Why keep living," he said, "since life is so bitter?"

He rushed over to them and might have killed them himself, except that a fit came over him that caused one of his hands to go limp. (He sometimes got such fits in sunny weather.) So he left them to kill themselves in whatever method they chose.

"Brother," said Christian, "what should we do? Wouldn't dying be better than to live like this?"

"Yes," Hopeful replied. "But to kill ourselves would be murder, which is against God's law. Besides, Giant Despair doesn't control everything. Others have been locked up here before, and surely some of them escaped. God may even decide to kill the giant. Or the giant might have another fit, and this time lose the use of both his hands. So let's be patient and hold out longer."

Toward evening Giant Despair came back, and was enraged to find them still alive. "It will be worse for you now than if you'd never been born," he said, before leaving them again.

Christian now was quite ready to die. But Hopeful said, "Brother, remember how brave you've been! Apollyon couldn't crush you, nor could everything you saw in the Valley of the Shadow of Death. At Vanity Fair you weren't afraid of chains or a cage or bloody death. What hardship and terror you've already endured! Surely you won't give in to fear now! Remember that I'm facing this with you, a far weaker man than you, and wounded by the giant just as you are. So let's be patient a little longer."

That night the giant's wife gave her husband more advice, and he followed it the next morning. He took the prisoners from the dungeon to the castleyard, where he showed them piles of skulls and bones. "These were once pilgrims like you," he said. "In my own good time I tore them to pieces. Ten days from now I'll do the same to you." He punched them all the way back to the dungeon.

That night the giant's wife advised him to search the prisoners in the morning for any picklocks they might be hiding. She didn't want them escaping.

The same night, Christian and Hopeful prayed together for hours. Suddenly Christian shouted, "What a fool I am, to lie here in a stinking dungeon when we can go free!" From under his shirt he pulled out a key hanging around his neck, a key called Promise. "I believe this key will open any lock in the castle," he said.

"Brother, let's do it," Hopeful agreed.

They tried it in the dungeon door, which flew open with ease. Then they tried it in the outer door to the castleyard. It opened as well. Next they faced an iron gate, which was harder to unlock, but finally it, too, swung open with the key. They were free to run.

The gate creaked when it opened, and Giant Despair woke up. He rose quickly to pursue his prisoners, but he felt his arms and legs become weak, and he couldn't chase them.

So Christian and Hopeful ran on. At Bypath Meadow they engraved a message in rocks, to warn future pilgrims about the wrong path leading to Doubting Castle and Giant Despair.

Then they were back on the King's highway, and were safe.

INTO THE RIVER

OW CHRISTIAN and Hopeful came to the Delectable Mountains, which Christian had first seen from the roof of the Palace Beautiful. Up into the mountains they climbed, up among gardens and grapevines and fruit trees and flowers and fountains of water. Near the top they found shepherds feeding their flocks. The pilgrims asked, "Is this the way to the Celestial City?"

"Yes, you're on your way."

"How far is it there?"

"Too far for anyone except those who truly want to go."

"Is the path safe or dangerous?"

"It's safe to those for whom God makes it safe; but sinners will stumble in the way."

The shepherds — whose names were Knowledge, Experience, Wakeful, and Sincere — took the pilgrims into their tents to eat and to rest, for it was late.

In the morning the shepherds asked Christian and Hopeful to walk with them on the mountains. They went first to a hill called Error. At the bottom of it, Christian and Hopeful saw what was left of several men dashed to pieces by a fall from the top.

They climbed another mountain called Caution. From there Christian and Hopeful could look down on several men walking among tombs. The men kept stumbling as if they were blind. The shepherds explained: "These are pilgrims who came to Bypath Meadow, and because the right path was rough, they chose an easier way. But it led straight to Doubting Castle and Giant Despair, who threw them in his dungeon. Then he put out their eyes and brought the pilgrims to those tombs, leaving them to wander there."

Next the shepherds took the pilgrims down to a door in the side of a hill. The door was opened. It was dark and smoky inside. Christian and Hopeful smelled sulfur, and heard the roar of a fire and the cry of someone being tortured. The shepherds explained that this was a shortcut to hell. It was the pathway taken there by hypocrites who seemed to be pilgrims, but were not.

Christian said to Hopeful, "We'll need to ask God for strength." To that the shepherds replied, "And you'll need to use that strength when you receive it."

At last the shepherds walked with the pilgrims to the end of the mountains. They led them up a high hill called Clear. From the top they saw the gates of the Celestial City.

As Christian and Hopeful were ready to leave, one of the shepherds gave them a map showing the rest of their journey. A second shepherd told them to beware of the Flatterer. A third warned them not to sleep on the Enchanted Ground. And the fourth one told them goodbye.

A little below the mountains they met a quick lad whose name was Ignorance. He had traveled along a crooked lane that came from the country of Conceit, and said he was going to the Celestial City.

"How do you expect to get in?" Christian asked.

"Just as other good people do," replied Ignorance. "I live a good life, I pay whatever I owe, I pray, and I give money to the poor."

"But you didn't come in at the narrow gate," said Christian, "so I'm afraid you won't be admitted to the city."

Ignorance replied, "You follow your religion, and I'll follow mine." So Ignorance stayed back as the pilgrims walked ahead.

Soon they entered a dark lane where they saw a man bound with seven strong ropes and being carried away by seven demons. Christian thought the man looked like someone he knew named Turnaway, from the town of Betrayal.

Further on the pilgrims came to a place where another path branched off from the one they were traveling, and it seemed just as straight and narrow as the other. They stood there wondering which way to take. Then a man came up wearing a robe of light. "Follow me," he said, "for I'm going to the Celestial City." So they followed him on the path that branched off. This new path curved slowly in the other direction, but the pilgrims didn't notice. Suddenly they became entangled in a net that was lying like a snare in the road. They couldn't get free. The white robe fell off the man they had followed, and they saw that he was the Flatterer.

They cried out for help. At last a Shining One came, carrying a whip. After he freed them and scolded them for following the Flatterer, he made them lie down and struck them with the whip. He spoke these words: "The Lord says, 'Those whom I love I rebuke and discipline.'" The pilgrims thanked him for his kindness. When they were back on the right path, they went along singing.

The next man they met on the road was named Atheist. "Where are you going," he asked them.

"To Mount Zion," Christian answered.

Atheist let out a great laugh. "How stupid you are to take on such a tiresome journey, and get nothing for all your trouble."

Christian replied, "Do you think we won't be let in when we get there?"

"Let in! Why, there is no Mount Zion. I once believed there was. But I've been seeking that city for twenty years now, and I've seen no more of it than I did the day I set out. I'm returning to my country to enjoy the things I loved before. If there ever was a Celestial City, I would have found it. Now I know it doesn't exist."

Christian then decided to test Hopeful. He asked him, "Is it true what this man says?"

"What!" Hopeful answered. "No City of Zion? Didn't we see it from the Delectable Mountains? Besides, we walk by faith. So let's ignore this Atheist, or else the man with the whip may catch us again." So they left Atheist, who went on his way laughing.

Christian and Hopeful next entered a place where they became drowsy. "I can scarcely hold open my eyes," Hopeful said. "Let's lie down and take a nap."

"No," said Christian. "If we sleep here we may never wake up. Don't you remember the shepherd warning us about the Enchanted Ground?"

They kept talking to keep one another awake. Hopeful told the story of how he had come to understand and believe in Jesus. Then he looked back and saw Ignorance still following at a distance. So the pilgrims stopped to let him catch up.

Christian asked him, "How is it now between God and your soul?"

Ignorance answered that he felt good about himself, that he had good thoughts about God and heaven, and that he had a good heart. But Christian explained that the only good thoughts are those that agree with God's Word, which says that our hearts are evil.

"I can never believe my heart is bad," Ignorance declared.

"Then you can never have a good thought about yourself," Christian answered. "Wake up, Ignorance, and see how sinful you are, then run to Jesus Christ to save you!"

"That's your belief, not mine," said Ignorance. Again he dropped back from the pilgrims and stayed behind.

Finally they passed over the Enchanted Ground and entered the land of Beulah, where the air is sweet and pleasant, the birds never stop singing, and the sun always shines. The pilgrims were there many days, and saw new flowers bloom each morning. Here they could see the Celestial City better than before. They saw its gold and its pearls and its precious stones. They were so hungry and thirsty to be there that it made them nearly sick.

I saw in my dream that they came to more gardens and fruit trees and grapevines.

When they ate the grapes, the sweetness made them sleep, but they talked in their sleep.

The Shining Ones often walked in that country, since it bordered on heaven. Christian and Hopeful met two of them dressed in robes that shone like gold. They said to the pilgrims, "You must face only two more difficulties before entering the city."

Christian and Hopeful asked the two men to go with them, and they agreed.

Now I saw that between the pilgrims and the Celestial Gate was a river with no bridge, and the river was very deep. The pilgrims were stunned to see it. But the men said to them, "You must go through it, or you cannot reach the gate."

Christian could see no way that he and Hopeful could escape the river.

"Is every part of it as deep as the rest?" he asked the Shining Ones.

"No," they answered. "You'll find it deep or shallow, depending on your faith in the King of this place."

So Christian and Hopeful stepped into the waters.

Welcomed Home

T ONCE Christian began sinking. The waves rushed over his head. He cried out to his friend Hopeful, who answered, "Be of good cheer, my brother. I feel the bottom, and it's solid."

Darkness and horror poured over Christian. "The sorrows of death sweep over me," he called. "Ah, my friend, I won't see the land that flows with milk and honey!" He could no longer remember any of the grace and encouragement God gave him along his journey. His mind and heart were filled only with fear that he would die in the river, and never walk through the gate on the other side. He remembered many sins he had committed, and thought he saw hobgoblins and evil spirits from the enemy.

Hopeful had all he could do trying to keep his brother's head above water, and to comfort him. "Brother," he said, "I see the gate! Men are standing beside it to welcome us!"

But Christian answered, "They're waiting for you, not me. You've been hopeful ever since I met you."

"And so have you," Hopeful said.

"No, my sins have snared me," cried Christian, "and God has forsaken me."

"No!" declared Hopeful. "God sent these waters only to test us, to see if we'll remember his goodness and depend on it."

Then I saw in my dream that Christian thought about this for a while. Then Hopeful said to him, "Be of good cheer. Jesus Christ keeps you safe!"

With that, Christian broke out in a loud voice, "Oh! I see him again! And he tells me, 'When you pass through the waters, I'll be with you; and when you pass through the rivers, they will not sweep over you.'"

Then they both took courage. And after this, their enemy was as still as a stone.

Christian found the bottom to stand upon. The waters now were shallow, so they both finished crossing over.

Hopeful and Christian climbed up from the river toward the gate. They walked with ease and speed. They found themselves up above the clouds, stepping through regions of air. The two Shining Ones came again to walk beside them.

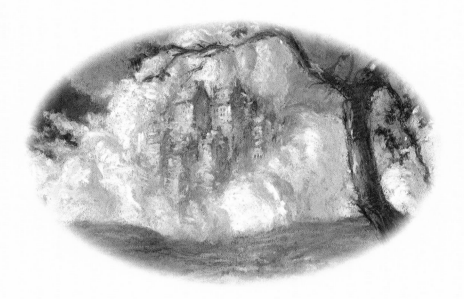

"You're coming to the Paradise of God," they said.

"What will we do there?" the pilgrims asked.

"You'll walk and talk with the King, every day of eternity. You'll receive rewards for all your work and all your sufferings. You'll have joy for all your sorrow. You must reap what you have sown, and will taste the fruit of all your prayers and tears. You'll wear crowns of gold, and white robes of glory and majesty. You'll have the sight and vision of the Holy One, for you shall see him as he is. You'll eat fruit from the tree of life. With praise and shouts and thanksgiving you'll never stop serving the Mighty One whom you desired so much to keep serving in the world. Your eyes will be delighted to see him, and your ears will always love his pleasant voice. You'll enjoy your friends again who have gone there before you, and with joy you'll welcome everyone who follows you there. You'll have armor to wear as you ride out with the King of glory, and you'll go with him as he soars on the wings of the wind. With the sound of the trumpet you'll return with him again to the city, and always be with him."

Now a great company of the heavenly host came out. The two Shining Ones said to them, "These are men who loved our Lord when they were in the world, and they left everything for his holy name, and he sent us to bring them here, so they may go and look into the face of their Redeemer with joy."

Then the heavenly host gave a great shout: "Blessed are those who are invited to the wedding supper of the Lamb!" The King's trumpeters also came out, dressed in white,

and made the heavens echo with their music. Seeing and hearing all the angels, it seemed to Christian and Hopeful as if they were already in heaven.

Now they saw the city itself as never before, and they heard the ringing of bells from inside it, to welcome them.

And in this way they came to the gate.

Over it, written in letters of gold, were these words:

> *Blessed are those who do his commandments,*
>
> *that they may have the right to the tree of life,*
>
> *and may enter through the gates into the city.*

I saw in my dream that the Shining Ones told the pilgrims to present themselves at the gate, where Enoch and Moses and Elijah and many others were waiting. The Shining Ones announced, "These pilgrims have come from the City of Destruction, because of their love for the King of this place."

Then Christian and Hopeful gave over their scrolls which they had received in the beginning, and these were carried in to the King. The King read them, then commanded, "Open the gates that the righteous may enter."

Now I saw in my dream that these two men proceeded through the gate. As they entered, they were changed, and their clothes became as gleaming as gold. They were given crowns to wear, and the bells in the city rang out again for joy. And the two men were told, "Enter into the joy of the Lord!"

Christian and Hopeful now began singing with a loud voice,

> *Blessing and honor and glory and power*
>
> *be unto him who sits on the throne*
>
> *and unto the Lamb, forever and ever!*

The city was shining like the sun. The streets were paved with gold, and were filled with men praising God. And I saw creatures with wings who kept calling to one other, "Holy, holy, holy is the Lord."

Then the gate was shut, now that Christian and Hopeful were inside. And after all I had seen, I wished that I myself was with them.

Now I turned my head to look back, and I saw Ignorance approaching the river. He soon got over it, for a man named Vain-Hope took him across in a ferryboat.

Ignorance climbed the hill that rose from the riverbank, but no one came out to meet him. When he reached the gate, he knocked, expecting to be quickly let in. Enoch and Moses and Elijah and the others looked over the gate and asked for his scroll.

Ignorance fumbled in his pockets.

"Don't you have one?" they asked.

He couldn't answer a word.

So they told the King about him. He called the two Shining Ones who had walked with Christian and Hopeful, and commanded them to tie up Ignorance hand and foot, and take him away. So they carried him far through the air to the door in the side of a hill. They threw Ignorance inside, and shut the door.

I saw therefore that there's a way to hell from the gates of heaven, as well as from the City of Destruction.

And so I awoke, and I looked — and it was all a dream.